CLF-C01: AWS Certified Cloud Practitioner

Exam Cram Notes

3rd Edition

Chapter 01: Cloud Concepts and Technology

Cloud Computing

Using a network of remote servers hosted on the internet to store, manage, and process data rather than using a local server or personal computer

Advantages of Cloud Computing

1. Trade capital expense for variable expense
2. Benefit from massive economies of scale
3. Stop guessing capacity
4. Increase speed and agility
5. Stop spending money on running/maintaining data centers
6. Go global in minutes

Types of Cloud Computing

- Infrastructure as a Service (IaaS)
- Platform as a Service (PaaS)
- Software as a Service (SaaS)

Cloud Computing Deployment Models

- **Cloud:** Third-party provider makes compute resources available to the public over the internet
- **Hybrid:** A mix of on-premises private cloud and third-party public cloud
- **On-Premises:** Uses the same legacy IT infrastructure and runs cloud resources within its own data center

Amazon Web Services Cloud Platform

Amazon Web Services (AWS) is a secure cloud services platform, offering compute power, database storage, content delivery, and other functionality on-demand.

The Cloud Computing Difference

- IT Assets Become Programmable Resources
- Global, Available, and Unlimited Capacity
- Higher Level Managed Services
- Security Built In

AWS Cloud Economics

Traditional Environment

Apart from hardware, storage, and compute costs. You have to manage other investments, such as:

- Capital expenditures
- Operational expenditures
- Staffing
- Opportunity costs
- Licensing
- Facilities overhead

Cloud Environment

Provides scalable and powerful computing solutions, reliable storage, and database technologies at lower costs with reduced complexity, and increased flexibility. When decoupled from the data center, you can:

- Decrease your TCO
- Reduce complexity
- Adjust capacity on the fly
- Reduce time to market
- Deploy quickly, even worldwide
- Increase efficiencies
- Innovate more
- Spend your resources strategically
- Enhance security

AWS Virtuous Cycle

AWS pricing philosophy is driven by a virtuous cycle. Lower prices mean more customers taking advantage of the platform, which results in further cost drops.

Amazon Route 53

Amazon Route 53 provides a highly available and scalable cloud DNS web service that effectively connects user requests to infrastructure running in AWS, such as EC2 instances, Elastic Load Balancers, or Amazon S3 buckets. It can also be used to route users to infrastructure outside of AWS. DNS (Domain Name System) is a globally distributed service that translates human-readable domain names like www.example.com to numeric

machine-readable IP addresses like 192.0.2.1 used by computers to connect to each other.

Applications

- DNS Management
- Traffic Management
- Availability Monitoring
- Domain Registration

AWS Cloud Deployment and Management Services

The deployment services are an easier way to deploy your application on the underlying infrastructure. AWS deployment tool handles the complexity of provisioning the AWS resources required for your application to run.

AWS Elastic Beanstalk

The fastest and simplest way to get an application up and running on AWS without worrying about managing the underlying infrastructure. Developers only need to upload their code while the service automates the deployment of all resources.

AWS CloudFormation

A powerful tool that offers the ability to script your infrastructure so that you can easily replicate your infrastructure stack quickly and as many times as you want.

AWS Quick Starts

Quick Starts are automated reference deployments like templates, built by AWS solutions architects and partners to assist you in deploying popular solutions of key technologies on AWS cloud, using AWS best practices for security and high availability.

AWS Global Infrastructure

AWS Cloud spans across 18 geographic Regions with 53 Availability Zones and 1 Local Region around the world, with further announced plans for expansion of the network.

Regions

The region is an independent and separate geographical area with multiple, physically separated, and isolated locations known as Availability Zones.

Availability Zones

An availability zone is simply a data center or a collection of data centers. Each Availability Zone in a Region has separate power, networking, and connectivity to reduce the chances of two zones failing simultaneously.

Edge Locations

Edge Locations are AWS sites deployed in major cities and highly populated areas across the globe and are used by AWS services such as AWS CloudFront to cache data and reduce latency for end-user access by using the Edge Locations as a global Content Delivery Network (CDN).

AWS Compute

Amazon Elastic Compute Cloud (Amazon EC2)

Amazon EC2 is a web service that provides secure, resizable cloud-based compute capacity in the form of EC2 instances, which are virtual servers in the cloud.

Pricing models for EC2 instances

- On-Demand Instances - allows you to pay a fixed rate by the hour (or by the second) with no long-term commitments or upfront payments
- Reserved Instances - provides you with capacity reservation over a 1-year or 3-years term resulting in significant discounts
- Spot Instances - enables you to bid your preferred price on spare EC2 instance capacity, providing you with even greater savings
- Dedicated Hosts - Dedicated Hosts are physical EC2 servers dedicated for your use

Recommended Uses Cases

- On-Demand Instances - Applications being developed or tested on Amazon EC2 for the first time
- Reserved Instances - Applications with steady-state or predictable usage, like web servers
- Spot Instances - Applications that have flexible start and end times
- Dedicated Hosts - Useful for regulatory requirements that may not support multi-tenant virtualization

EC2 Instance Types

Range of instance types optimized for different use cases

- General Purpose – T2, M5
- Compute Optimized – C5

- Storage Optimized – H1, I3, D2
- Memory Optimized – X1, R4
- Accelerated Computing – P3, G3, F1

AWS Storage

Amazon Simple Storage Service (Amazon S3)

Amazon S3 is object storage designed to store, access, and retrieve any type and amount of data over the internet through a simple web service interface.

Amazon S3 Basics

- Buckets - Container for objects stored in S3
- Objects - Fundamental entities stored in S3
- Keys - Unique identifier of an object in a bucket

Amazon S3 Storage Classes

- For Frequently Accessed Objects
  - Standard S3
  - Reduced Redundancy Storage
- For Infrequently Accessed Objects
  - S3 Standard – Infrequent Access
  - S3 One Zone – Infrequent Access

Amazon S3 Fundamental Characteristics

- Security & Access Management
  - Flexible Access Control Mechanism
    1. IAM Policies
    2. Access Control Lists (ACLs)
    3. Bucket Policies
    4. Query String Authentication
  - Encryption
  - Versioning
- Storage Management
  - Object Tagging
  - Data Lifecycle Management
  - Cross-Region Replication
- Data Transfer - S3 charges for the following:
  - Amount of storage
  - Number of requests
  - Storage management pricing
  - Data transfer pricing
  - Transfer Acceleration

Amazon Glacier

An exceptionally low-cost storage service, offering durable, secure, and flexible storage for data archival and long-term backup. It provides three options for access to archives to cater to varying retrieval needs:

- Expedited retrieval – typically returns data in 1 to 5 minutes
- Standard retrievals – returns between 3 to 5 hours
- Bulk retrievals – returns a large amount of data within 5 to 12 hours

Amazon Elastic Block Store (Amazon EBS)

Provides persistent block storage volumes for use with Amazon EC2 instances in the AWS Cloud.

Amazon EBS Volume Types

- General Purpose SSD(gp2)
- Provisioned IOPS SSD (io1)
- Throughput Optimized HDD (st1)
- Cold HDD (sc1)

Amazon EBS Magnetic Volumes

Previous generation volumes backed by hard disk drives (HDDs). Ideal for workloads with smaller datasets where data is infrequently accessed and applications where primary importance is of lowest storage cost and not performance consistency.

Identity Access Management (IAM)

IAM manages authentication and authorization by controlling who is signed in and has permission to utilize the resources.

IAM Features

IAM uses access control concepts such as Users, Groups, Roles, and Policies to control which users can access specific services, the kinds of actions they can perform, and which resources are available to them

- **IAM User** – IAM User is a unique identity with limited access to an AWS account and its resources, as defined by their IAM permissions and policies
- **Group -** Group is a collection of IAM users that can be granted permissions that makes it easier to manage permissions for those users
- **IAM Role** - IAM role lets you define a set of permissions to access the resources that a user or service needs, but the permissions are not attached to a specific IAM user or group.
- **Policy -** IAM policy is a rule or set of rules defining the operations allowed/denied to be performed

on an AWS resource. Permissions are granted through policies.

IAM Functionality
- Manage IAM users and their access
- Manage IAM roles and their permissions
- Manage federated users and their permissions

IAM Best Practices
- Create individual Users
- Use Groups
- Use policies to assign permissions
- Monitor activity in your AWS account
- Configure a strong password policy
- Enable MFA
- Use Roles to share access
- Rotate security credentials regularly
- Lock your AWS Account Root User access keys and reduce or remove the use of root

IAM Credential Report

The IAM Credential Report lists all AWS account user details within your organization. It includes account status such as various credentials including passwords, access keys, and MFA. You can download or generate a credential report. The IAM Credential Report can help you with your auditing and compliance operations. The report may be used to check the impact of credential lifecycle requirements like password and access key rotation. You can provide a credential report to the auditor directly or permit them to download the report directly. You can generate the credential report once every four hours.

AWS Networking & Content Delivery

Amazon Virtual Private Cloud (Amazon VPC)

Amazon VPC lets you provision a logically isolated section of the AWS cloud where you can launch AWS resources in a virtual network that you define.

Components of Amazon VPC
- A Virtual Private Cloud
- Subnet
- Internet Gateway
- NAT Gateway
- Hardware VPN Connection
- Virtual Private Gateway
- Customer Gateway

- Router
- Peering Connection
- VPC Endpoints
- Egress-only Internet Gateway

Amazon CloudFront

Amazon CloudFront is a global content delivery network (CDN) service that securely delivers data, videos, applications, and APIs to end users with low latency and high transfer speeds.

- If the content is already in the edge location with the lowest latency, CloudFront instantly delivers it.
- If the content is not currently in that edge location, CloudFront retrieves it from the Origin.

Origin: Source of the files that the CDN will distribute

Distribution: Name given to the CDN, consisting of a collection of edge locations

Amazon CloudFront Benefits
- Global, Growing Content Delivery Network
- Secure Content at the Edge
- Programmable CDN
- High Performance
- Cost Effective
- Deep Integration with Key AWS Services

Elastic Load Balancing

Distributes incoming application traffic across multiple EC2 instances to provide seamless necessary load balancing capacity

Elastic Load Balancing supports three types of load balancers:

- Application Load Balancer – Makes routing decisions at the application layer
- Network Load Balancer – Makes routing decisions at the transport layer
- Classic Load Balancer – Makes routing decisions at the transport layer or the application layer

AWS Compute

Amazon Elastic Compute Cloud (Amazon EC2)

Amazon EC2 is a web service that provides secure, resizable cloud-based compute capacity in the form of EC2 instances, which are virtual servers in the cloud.

Pricing models for EC2 instances

- **On-Demand Instances** - allows you to pay a fixed rate by the hour (or by the second) with no long-term commitments or upfront payments
- **Reserved Instances** - provides you with capacity reservation over a 1-year or 3-years term resulting in significant discounts
- **Spot Instances** - enables you to bid your preferred price on spare EC2 instance capacity, providing you with even greater savings
- **Dedicated Hosts** - Dedicated Hosts are physical EC2 servers dedicated for your use

Recommended Uses Cases

- **On-Demand Instances** - Applications being developed or tested on Amazon EC2 for the first time
- **Reserved Instances** - Applications with steady-state or predictable usage, like web servers
- **Spot Instances** - Applications that have flexible start and end times
- **Dedicated Hosts** - Useful for regulatory requirements that may not support multi-tenant virtualization

EC2 Instance Types

Range of instance types optimized for different use cases

- General Purpose – T2, M5
- Compute Optimized – C5
- Storage Optimized – H1, I3, D2
- Memory Optimized – X1, R4
- Accelerated Computing – P3, G3, F1

AWS Database

Amazon Relational Database Service (Amazon RDS)

Amazon RDS is a managed relational database service that makes it easy to set up, operate, and scale a relational database in the AWS cloud.

Amazon RDS Supported Databases

- Amazon Aurora
- MySQL
- MariaDB
- Oracle
- Microsoft SQL Server
- PostgreSQL

Amazon RDS Key Features

- **Multi-Availability Zones** - Provision and manages a standby replica automatically in a different Availability Zone. Used for disaster recovery
- **Read Replicas** - Database updates on the source DB instance are replicated to the Read Replica. Used for performance improvement

Amazon Aurora

Amazon Aurora is a MySQL and PostgreSQL-compatible relational database engine built for the cloud that combines the speed and availability of high-end commercial databases with the easiness and cost-effectiveness of open source databases.

Amazon DynamoDB

Amazon DynamoDB is a fully managed, fast, and flexible NoSQL database service for applications that require consistent and predictable performance with seamless scalability.

DynamoDB Accelerator (DAX)

Amazon DynamoDB Accelerator (DAX) is a fully managed, highly available, in-memory cache that can reduce DynamoDB response times from milliseconds to microseconds.

Data Warehouse

- This is a special type of relational database, which is optimized for the analysis and reporting of large amounts of data

- It is used to combine transactional data from disparate sources so that they are available for analysis and decision-making

- Running complex transactions and queries on the production database creates massive overheads and require an immense quantity of processing power, which is why data warehousing is needed

- An AWS example of a Data Warehouse is Amazon Redshift

Amazon Redshift

Amazon Redshift is a fast, fully managed, petabyte-scale data warehouse that analyzes large data sets using standard SQL and existing Business Intelligence (BI) tools.

Search
- A search service is used to index and search data, both in structured and free text format
- A search service is required because sophisticated search functionality typically outgrows the capabilities of relational or NO SQL databases

Graph Database

Graph databases are designed specifically to store and navigate relationships.

Non-Relational Databases
- These are often called NoSQL databases
- They trade the query and transaction capabilities of relational databases for a more flexible data model
- They utilize a variety of data models, including graphs, key-value pairs, and JSON documents
- An AWS example of this is Amazon DynamoDB

Managing Increasing Volumes of Data
- Managing increasing volumes of data is simply an architectural approach to storing massive amounts of data in a centralized location.

Removing Single Points of Failure

A system needs to be widely available to withstand any failure of either individual or multiple components, for example, hard disks, servers, and network links. Resiliency should be built across multiple services as well as in multiple availability zones to automate the recovery and reduce disruption at every layer of the architecture.

- **Introducing Redundancy** - You can introduce redundancy by creating multiple resources for the same task. Redundancy can be implemented in either standby or active mode. In standby mode, functionality is recovered through a secondary resource while the initial resource remains unavailable. In active mode, requests are distributed to multiple redundant computing resources when any single one fails.
- **Detect Failure**- Processes of detection and reaction to failure should both be automated as much as possible, by configuring health checks and masking failure by routing traffic to healthy endpoints using services like ELB and Amazon Route53. Auto Scaling can also be configured to replace unhealthy nodes using the Amazon EC2 auto-recovery feature or services such as AWS OpsWorks and AWS Elastic Beanstalk.
- **Durable Data Storage** – Durable data storage is vital for data availability and integrity and can be achieved by introducing redundant copies of data. The three most-often used modes of replication are; Asynchronous Replication, Synchronous Replication, and Quorum-based Replication.

AWS On-Premises Services

These are the AWS services that you can use on-premises in your own datacenters or inside your corporate headquarters.

Snowball

Snowball was the first AWS on-premises service. It is just like a gigantic disk. You essentially get Snowball delivered to your headquarters, load up all your data on it, and then ship it back to Amazon.

Snowball Edge

Snowball Edge is very similar to a Snowball except that it also has a CPU, and it is a computer with storage, and it allows you to deploy Lambda functions on-premises.

Storage Gateway

The AWS Storage Gateway is a hybrid cloud service that is very similar to Snowball except that it stays on premise at all times. It can either be physical or virtual. It is mostly used to cache your files inside your datacenter or your headquarters and then replicate those files directly to S3.

CodeDeploy

The AWS CodeDeploy is a way of deploying your code to EC2 instances, but you can deploy your code to your on-premises web servers as well. AWS CodeDeploy makes it easier for you rapidly release new features, helps you avoid downtime during application deployment, and handles the complexity of updating your applications.

Opsworks

You can use Opsworks to deploy your application code to both EC2 instances inside the AWS cloud as well as to your own on-premises.

IoT Greengrass

AWS IoT Greengrass allows you to create intelligent device software quickly and easily. Local processing, communications, data management, and machine learning inference are all possible with AWS IoT Greengrass, which also includes pre-built components to speed up application development. AWS IoT Greengrass allows you to link your edge devices to any AWS service as well as third-party services in a secure manner.

Autoscaling

AWS Autoscaling monitors your applications and automatically adjusts capacity to maintain steady, predictable performance at the lowest possible cost. Using AWS AutoScaling, you can set upscaling for multiple resources across multiple services in minutes. AWS AutoScaling provides a simple, powerful user interface that lets you build scaling plans for Amazon EC2 instances and Spot Fleets, Amazon ECS tasks, Amazon DynamoDB tables, and Amazon Aurora Replicas.

Register a Domain Name

Amazon Route 53 is a highly available and scalable cloud Domain Name System (DNS) web service. It is designed to give developers and businesses an extremely reliable and cost-effective way to route end users to Internet applications by translating names like www.example.com into the numeric IP addresses like 192.0.2.1 that computers use to connect. Amazon Route 53 is fully compliant with IPv6 as well.

Elastic Beanstalk

AWS Elastic Beanstalk is an easy-to-use service for deploying and scaling web applications and services developed with Java, .NET, PHP, Node.js, Python, Ruby, Go, and Docker on familiar servers such as Apache, Nginx, Passenger, and IIS.

AWS Cloud Architecture Design Principles

Scalability

Two ways to scale an IT architecture, vertically and horizontally.

- **Scale Vertically** - increase specifications such as RAM, CPU, IO, or networking capabilities

- **Scale Horizontally** - increase number of resources such as adding more hard drives to a storage array or adding more servers to support an application

Disposable Resources Instead of Fixed Servers

Treat servers and other components as temporary disposable resources, launch as many as needed, and use them as long as you need them

- **Instantiating Compute Resources** - keep the process of configuration and coding as an automated and repeatable process to avoid human errors and long lead times
- **Infrastructure as Code** - AWS assets are programmable. Deploy the infrastructure across multiple regions repeatedly without the need to go and provision everything manually

Automation

Automate using various AWS automation technologies wherever possible to improve the system's stability and efficiency of the organization.

Loose Coupling

Design systems with reduced interdependency. Break them down into smaller loosely coupled components

- Well-Defined Interfaces
- Service Discovery
- Asynchronous Integration
- Graceful Failure

Services, Not Servers

Leverage the compute, storage, database, analytics, application, and deployment services of AWS to increase developer productivity and operational efficiency

- **Managed Services** - Power applications by using AWS managed services that include databases, machine learning, analytics, queuing, search, email, notifications, and many more
- **Serverless Architectures** – reduce the operational complexity of running applications. Event-driven and synchronous services can both be built without managing any server infrastructure

Databases

AWS managed database services to remove constraints that come with licensing costs and the ability to support diverse database engines. Database technologies offered by AWS include:

- **Relational Databases** - Amazon Relational Database Service (RDS) and Amazon Aurora
- **Non-Relational Databases** – Amazon DynamoDB
- **Data Warehouse** – Amazon Redshift
- **Search -** Amazon CloudSearch and Amazon Elasticsearch (ES)

Removing Single Points of Failure

Build resiliency across multiple services as well as multiple availability zones to automate the recovery and reduce disruption at every layer of the architecture by:

- Introduce redundancy
- Detect failure
- Having durable data storage
- Automated multi-data center resilience
- Fault isolation and traditional horizontal scaling

Optimize for Cost

Reduce capital expenses by benefiting from the AWS economies of scale by

- Right sizing
- Implementing elasticity
- Take advantage of a variety of purchasing options

Caching

Storing previously calculated data for future use improves application performance and increases the cost efficiency of implementation. This can be done by:

- Application Data Caching
- Edge Caching

Security

Improve security using security tools and techniques:

- Utilize AWS features for defense in depth
- Offload security responsibility to AWS
- Reduce privileged access
- Apply security as code
- Enable real-time auditing

Global AWS Services

AWS provides a lot of services and these services are either Global, regional, or specific to the availability zone and cannot be accessed outside.

IAM (Identity Access Management)

When we create a user, a group or a role, or a policy that applies globally, there is no use for a specific region. Using IAM, you can create and manage AWS users and groups, and use permissions to permit and deny their access to AWS resources.

Route53

Route53 is used when you go and register a domain name. It is not tied to any particular region. Amazon Route 53 is fully compliant with IPv6 as well.

CloudFront

The Amazon CloudFront is a quick Content Delivery Network (CDN) administration that safely conveys information, recordings, applications, and APIs to clients universally with low latency, high transfer speeds, all within a developer-friendly environment.

SNS (Simple Notification Service)

Simple Notification Service (SNS) is a fully managed messaging service for both Application-to-Application (A2A) and Application-to-Person (A2P) communication.

SES (Simple Email Service)

Simple Email Service (SES) is a cost-effective, flexible, and scalable email service that enables developers to send mail from within any application.

CloudWatch 101

Amazon CloudWatch is all about monitoring performance. CloudWatch is a service for monitoring your AWS resources, as well as the applications you run on AWS.

Service Health Dashboard

A service health dashboard is a way of seeing the health of the different AWS services. This dashboard regularly showcases updated data about service availability in the region. It provides:

1. **Overview of all regions:** Shows all regions and the health of all AWS services in those regions.

2. **Daily historical regions:** You can review all historical information for each AWS service on a per-day basis.

3. **RSS feeds:** You can subscribe to RSS feeds and get immediate notifications if a specific service in a particular region goes down.

Personal Health Dashboard

Personal Health Dashboard is a dashboard that is personalized for you. You can view the performance and availability of the AWS services underlying your AWS resources. Hence, the advantages of a Personal Health Dashboard are:

- **Personalized for you:** The personalized health dashboard offers an overview of the AWS services that you use and whether or not they are having any availability issues.

- **Relevant up-to-date information:** The dashboard displays up-to-date information on the status of your AWS services and provides proactive notifications as to any scheduled activities.

Chapter 02: Security in the Cloud

AWS Cloud Security

Security in the cloud is much like security in traditional on-premises data centers, only without the costs of maintaining facilities and hardware. The security provided includes protecting critical information from theft, data leakage, integrity and deletion. In the cloud environment, the cloud provider manages the physical servers or storage devices while the customer uses software-based security tools to monitor and protect the flow of information through the cloud resources.

Benefits of AWS Security

- Keep your data safe
- Meet compliance requirements
- Save money
- Scale quickly

AWS Compliance and AWS Artifacts:

AWS Compliance

AWS supports more security standards and compliance certifications than any other offering, including PCI-DSS, HIPAA/HITECH, FedRAMP, GDPR, FIPS 140-2, and NIST 800-171, helping customers satisfy compliance requirements for virtually every regulatory agency around the globe.

To view the different compliance reports of AWS, you can go to **aws.amazon.com/compliance/programs/**

Globally, we have ISO 27001. We also have SOC 1, SOC 2, and SOC 3, as well as PCI DSS. PCI DSS is an online payment standard. AWS is PCI DSS compliant up to the infrastructure layer. This does not mean that you are automatically PCI DSS compliant. You have gap audits, that scrutinize your EC2 instances. It checks whether you have your security groups open, or if you have secured your RDS instances.

AWS Artifact

AWS Artifact features a comprehensive list of access-controlled documents relevant to compliance and security in the AWS cloud. For example, you can get compliance documents for the AWS Workbook for Korean Financial Services Institute. AWS Artifact means getting documentation around compliance.

AWS Shared Responsibility Model

AWS manages the security of the cloud; security in the cloud is the responsibility of the customer.

AWS Security Responsibilities

AWS operates, manages, and controls components of the host operating system and virtualization layer down to the physical security of the facilities in which the services operate. AWS is also responsible for the security configuration of its managed services.

Customer Security Responsibilities

AWS customers retain control over their data and are responsible to protect confidentiality, integrity, and availability of their data in the cloud. They are in charge of the management of their operating system (including updates and security patches) as well as the configuration of the AWS-provided security group firewall.

AWS Global Infrastructure Security

AWS global infrastructure utilizes security best practices along with a range of security compliance standards. It monitors and protects the underlying infrastructure 24x7 using redundant and layered controls, continuous validation and testing, and extensive automation. AWS ensures replication of these controls in each new data center or service.

AWS Compliance Program

AWS computing environments are continuously audited, with certifications from accreditation bodies across geographies and verticals, including ISO 27001, FedRAMP, DoD CSM, and PCI DSS. By operating in an accredited environment, customers reduce the scope and cost of audits they need to perform. AWS Compliance programs are divided into three areas:

Certifications / Attestations

Compliance certifications and attestations are assessed by a third-party, independent auditor and result in a certification, audit report or an attestation of compliance. Major certification and attestations that you need to be aware of for this course include ISO 27001, PCI DSS Level 1, SOC 1, SOC 2, and SOC 3.

Laws, Regulations, and Privacy

AWS customers are still responsible for complying with applicable compliance laws and regulations. The main one you should be aware of is HIPAA.

Alignments / Frameworks

Compliance alignments and frameworks consist of published security or compliance requirements for a specific industry or function. The one to focus on is G-Cloud [UK].

AWS Access Management

Three ways of accessing AWS services:

- The AWS Management Console
- The Command Line Interface
- Software Development Kits (SDKs)

Security Support

AWS provides its customers with a variety of tools and features to assist them in achieving security objectives and maintaining an optimized environment.

AWS WAF

AWS WAF provides protection to web applications against common web exploits that disrupt application accessibility, compromise security, or consume undue resources. It prevents common attack patterns like SQL injection and Cross-Site Scripting (XSS) efficiently by monitoring the HTTP and HTTPS requests

AWS Shield

AWS Shield is a managed protection service that safeguards web applications running on AWS against Distributed Denial of Service (DDoS) attacks. There are two tiers of AWS Shield:

- **Standard -** Protects against commonly occurring Infrastructure (OSI layer 3 and layer 4) attacks such as SYN/UDP Floods, Reflection attacks, etc.
- **Advanced** - Delivers enhanced protection against larger and more sophisticated attacks by

flow-based monitoring of network traffic and active application scrutiny to notify of DDoS attacks in near real-time

AWS Inspector

Amazon Inspector is an automated security assessment service that assists in improving the security and compliance of the applications running on Amazon EC2

AWS Trusted Advisor

AWS Trusted Advisor is an online resource for optimizing your AWS environment by following AWS best practices.

Trusted Advisor performs a list of checks in the following four categories:

- Cost Optimization
- Security
- Fault Tolerance
- Performance

AWS Trusted Advisor is available to the customers in two different forms:

- **Core Checks and Recommendations** - Available to all AWS customers at no additional cost. Access to seven core checks to improve security and performance
- **Full Trusted Advisor** - Available with Business and Enterprise Support Plans only. Access to a complete set of checks to help optimize your entire AWS infrastructure.

CloudTrail

CloudTrail monitors API calls in the AWS platform. CloudTrail is like a CCTV camera, it records everything that is going on in your AWS environment. Furthermore, it gives you increased visibility into your AWS environment by recording AWS Management Console actions and API calls. When creates a new user, or a group, or a role, or an EC2 instance, or an S3 bucket, AWS CloudTrail is going to record that and you can identify which users and accounts called AWS, the source IP address from which the calls were made and when the calls occurred. And that is all will saved into S3.

CloudWatch Vs AWS Config

CloudWatch

CloudWatch is an online monitoring service to monitor your AWS resources, as well as the applications that you run on AWS.

We use CloudWatch a lot with EC2, which are virtual machines in the clouds, and they sit on virtual machines. And the host (VM) reports back to CloudWatch.

Host Level Metrics consists of:

- CPU utilization
- Network utilization
- Disk utilization
- Status check of your EC2 instance

Custom metrics with CloudWatch:

- RAM utilization
- Check storage on EBS volumes
- Check the number of people that are logged into your WordPress site etc.

AWS Config

AWS Config provides a detailed view of the configuration of your AWS resources in your AWS account. This includes how the resources are related to one another, and how they were configured in the past. With this, you can see the configurations and relationships change over time.

AWS Penetration Testing

The penetration test, also known as a "pentest," is a simulated cyberattack against your computer system to check for exploitable vulnerabilities.

Penetration testing can be carried out against your AWS infrastructure without prior approval for eight services:

- Amazon EC2
- Amazon Aurora
- Amazon RDS
- AWS CloudFront
- AWS Elastic Beanstalk
- AWS Lambda
- AWS API Gateway
- AWS LightSail

KMS VS HSM

What is AWS KMS?

KMS stands for Key Management Service. AWS Key Management Service makes it easy for you to create and manage cryptographic keys and control their use across a wide range of AWS services applications.

1. KMS is a regional service that performs secure management and does encryption and decryption for your data.
2. Manages your Customer Master Keys (CMKs).
3. Is ideal for S3 objects, database passwords, API keys that are stored in systems manager parameter store, etc.
4. It is used to encrypt and decrypt data up to four kilobytes in size.
5. It is integrated with most AWS services. It is integrated with AWS CloudTrail in order to provide you with logs of all key usage to help meet your regulatory and compliance needs.
6. KMS is on shared hardware.

What is AWS CloudHSM?

HSM stands for hardware security module. AWS CloudHSM is a cloud-based hardware security module that enables you to easily generate and use your own encryption keys on the AWS Cloud.

1. HSM is a dedicated security module for you. It is not multitenant.
2. It complies with FIPS 140-2 level 3. FIPS stands for federal information processing standards, it is a US government computer security standard that essentially specifies the requirements for cryptography modules.
3. It is a single-tenant, dedicated hardware, multi-AZ cluster.
4. To avoid a situation where your CloudHSM dies and you suddenly cannot decrypt your data, you can deploy it across multi-availability zones in clusters. You can have two or three units in different availability zones as well. But, doing this is also going to add to your cost.

Secret Manager vs. Parameter Store

What is Parameter Store?

Parameter Store is an AWS service that stores strings. It can store secret data and non-secret data alike. Secrets stored in Parameter Store are secure strings, encrypted with a customer-specific AWS KMS key.

Parameter store is a component of AWS systems manager or S-S-M. It is secure serverless storage for configuration and secrets.

For example, you can store passwords and database strings in it and connect easily with the MySQL server database. The values of the string are stored via encrypted KMS and plain text as well. You can also set a time to live (TTL) to get an alert about the to expire of the passwords.

What is a Secret Manager?

AWS Secret Manager helps you protect secrets needed to access your applications, services, and IT resources. The service enables you to easily rotate, manage, and retrieve database credentials, API keys, and other secrets throughout their lifecycle.

Secrets Manager is expensive. You are charged per secrets stored, and you are also charged on a 10,000 API call basis. Some advantages of a secret manager are:

- ➢ Automatically rotate secrets
- ➢ Apply the new key/passwords in RDS for you
- ➢ Generate random secrets

Amazon GuardDuty

Amazon GuardDuty is a threat detection service that continuously monitors for malicious activity and unauthorized behavior to protect your AWS accounts, workloads, and data stored in Amazon S3. It is an intelligent and cost-effective option for continuous threat detection in AWS. GuardDuty uses machine learning algorithms for anomaly detection.

AWS Control Tower

AWS Control Tower provides the easiest way to set up and govern a secure, multi-account AWS environment, called a landing zone. It can be used for setting up multiple AWS accounts at once. It allows you to provision multiple AWS counts in just a few minutes and those accounts will conform to your company policies. It is used for large enterprises with multiple AWS accounts.

AWS Security Hub

Security Hub collects security data from across AWS accounts, services, and supported third-party partner products. It helps you analyze your security trends and identify the highest priority security issues.

Security Hub provides a single place that aggregates, organizes, and prioritizes your security alerts and findings from multiple AWS services, such as Amazon Guard Duty, Amazon Inspector, Amazon Macie, IAM, Access Analyzer, AWS Firewall Manager, etc. across multiple AWS accounts.

Benefits

- Save time with aggregated findings
- Improve security posture with automated checks
- Quickly take action on findings

Athena vs. Macie

Amazon Athena

Amazon Athena is an interactive query service, which makes it easy to analyze data in S3 using standard SQL. The benefits of Amazon Athena are:

- It allows you to quickly query on structured, semi-structured, and structured data stores in S3.
- It is a serverless-based service.
- It is designed to provide fast performance for large data sets.
- It is designed for 99.99999% durability.

Amazon Macie

Amazon Macie is a powerful security and compliance enabling service that sits within the identity, management, and compliance category of the AWS management console. The main function of the service is to provide automatic detection, classifying, and identifying the data that is stored in the AWS account. Macie is a service that uses machine learning to allow your data to be actively reviewed as different actions taken within the AWS account.

Personally Identifiable Information

PII is personally identifiable information.

- It is personal data used to establish an individual's identity.
- This data could be exploited by criminals used in identity theft and then financial fraud.
- Home address, email address, SSN
- Passport number, drivers license number
- D.O.B, phone number, bank account, credit card number

Chapter 03: Advanced AWS Concepts

Introduction

AWS provides building blocks that can support virtually any workload. It offers services that are designed to work together to build sophisticated scalable applications. You have access to highly durable storage, low-cost compute, management tools, high-performance databases, and more. All this is available without up-front cost, and you pay for only what you use. These services help organizations move faster, lower IT costs, and scale easily.

AWS is trusted by the largest enterprises and the hottest start-ups to power a wide variety of workloads, including web and mobile applications, game development, data processing and warehousing, storage, archive, and many others.

AI Services - Lex, Polly, Transcribe, Rekognition

AWS offers a family of intelligent services that provide cloud-native machine learning and deep learning technologies to address your different use cases and needs. For developers looking to add managed AI services to their applications, AWS brings Natural Language Understanding (NLU) and Automatic Speech Recognition (ASR) with Amazon Lex, visual search and image recognition with Amazon Rekognition, Text-to-Speech (TTS) with Amazon Polly, and developer-focused machine learning with Amazon Machine Learning.

Amazon Lex

Lex is what powers Amazon's Alexa. Lex is a service that allows you to build conversational chatbots that can either be powered via voice or via text.

- Amazon Lex provides an easy-to-use console to guide you through the process of creating your own chatbot or conversational interface in minutes.

- With Amazon Lex, you can easily build, test, and deploy your chatbot everywhere across all your channels and platforms. This includes mobile devices, web apps, and chat services such as Facebook Messenger, Slack, etc.

- With Amazon Lex, there are no upfront costs or minimum fees. You are only charged for the text or speech requests that are made. Amazon Lex's pay-as-you-go pricing and low cost per request make it a cost-effective way to build conversational interfaces anywhere.

Amazon Polly

Amazon Polly is a service that turns text into lifelike speech, allowing you to create applications that talk and build entirely new categories of speech-enabled products. Polly's Text-to-Speech service uses advanced deep learning technologies to synthesize natural-sounding human speech.

Amazon Transcribe

Amazon Transcribe uses a deep learning process called automatic speech recognition to convert speech to text quickly and accurately. Amazon Transcribe can be used to transcribe customer service calls, automate subtitling, and generate metadata for media assets to create a fully searchable archive.

Amazon Rekognition

Amazon Rekognition is a way of converting images into tags or texts. It is a way of allowing your software to see the image. You can upload an image and Rekognition will tell you what it thinks the image is with a certain degree of confidence.

With Amazon Rekognition, you can identify objects, people, text, scenes, and activities in images and videos, as well as detect any inappropriate content. Amazon Rekognition also provides highly accurate facial analysis and facial search capabilities that you can use to detect, analyze, and compare faces for a wide variety of user

verification, people counting, and public safety use cases.

EC2 Licensing

There are different types of EC2 pricing models:

1. **On-Demand:** Pay by the second/hour depending on the instance type.
2. **Reserved:** Pay more upfront with one- to three-year commitments, but get a lot more savings than with on-demand instances.
3. **Spot:** A Spot instance is an unused EC2 instance that is available for less than the on-demand price. Spot instances run whenever the capacity is available and the maximum price per hour for your request exceeds the Spot price. It is not good if you need consistent computing, such as web servers; for example, when you want your web servers to always be on so they can answer requests. Spot price instances can be terminated by AWS if the price per hour drops below the spot price.
4. **Dedicated Host:** Used for where you have special licensing requirements.

Amazon EC2 Dedicated Hosts allow you to use your eligible software licenses in AWS, you get the flexibility and effectiveness of using your own licenses, but with the resiliency, simplicity, and elasticity of AWS.

Different Compute Service

EC2

Amazon Elastic Compute Cloud (Amazon EC2) is a web service that provides secure, resizable compute capacity in the cloud. It is designed to make web-scale computing easier for developers.

LightSail

Amazon LightSail is designed to be the easiest way to launch and manage a virtual private server with AWS. LightSail plans include everything you need to jumpstart your project – a virtual machine, SSD-based storage, data transfer, DNS management, and a static IP address – for a low, predictable price.

Lambda

AWS Lambda lets you run code without provisioning or managing servers. You pay only for the compute time you consume.

Batch

AWS Batch enables developers to easily and efficiently run hundreds of thousands of batch computing jobs on AWS.

Elastic Beanstalk

AWS Elastic Beanstalk is an easy-to-use service for deploying and scaling web applications and services developed with Java, .NET, PHP, Node.js, Python, etc., on familiar servers.

Serverless Application Repository

This allows you to deploy pre-provision serverless applications such as Alexa skills.

AWS Outposts

AWS Outposts bring native AWS services, infrastructure, and operating models to virtually any data center, co-location space, or on-premises facility.

EC2 Image Builder

EC2 image builder helps you build your own custom EC2 images for Linux and Windows.

AWS Networking & Content Delivery

Amazon Virtual Private Cloud (Amazon VPC)

Amazon VPC lets you provision a logically isolated section of the AWS cloud from which you can launch AWS resources to a virtual network that you define. You have complete control over your virtual networking environment, including the selection of IP address ranges, the creation of subnets, and the configuration of route tables and network gateways.

A Virtual Private Cloud is a cloud computing model that offers an on-demand configurable pool of shared computing resources located within a public cloud environment while providing a certain level of isolation from other users of the public cloud. Since the cloud is only accessible to a single client in a VPC model, it offers privacy with greater control and a secure environment in which only the specified client can operate.

Components of Amazon VPC

- A Virtual Private Cloud

- Subnet
- Internet Gateway
- NAT Gateway
- Hardware VPN Connection
- Virtual Private Gateway
- Customer Gateway
- Router
- Peering Connection
- VPC Endpoints
- Egress-only Internet Gateway

Features & Benefits

Multiple Connectivity Options:

- Connect directly to the Internet using public subnets
- Connect to the Internet using Network Address Translation using private subnets
- Connect securely to your corporate datacenter
- Connect privately to other VPCs
- Privately connect to AWS Services without using an Internet gateway, NAT or firewall proxy through a VPC Endpoint
- Privately connect to SaaS solutions supported by AWS PrivateLink
- Privately connect your internal services across different accounts and VPCs

Secure:

- Advanced security features such as security groups and network access control lists enable inbound and outbound filtering at the instance level and at the subnet level
- Store data in Amazon S3 and restrict access so that it is only accessible from instances in your VPC
- For additional isolation, launch dedicated instances which run on hardware dedicated to a single customer

Simple:

- Setup VPC quickly and easily using the AWS Management Console
- Easily select common network setups that best match your needs

- Subnets, IP ranges, route tables, and security groups are automatically created using VPC Wizard

Scalability & Reliability:

- Amazon VPC provides all of the benefits of the AWS platform

Connecting On-premises to Your VPC

We can connect our on-premises environments to AWS. It could be your own datacenter or head office. There are two different ways of doing this and there is even a way to combine both methodologies.

Connect using VPN

You can create a hardware Virtual Private Network (VPN) connection between your corporate datacenter and your VPC leveraging the AWS cloud as an extension of your corporate network and datacenter. VPN is just a way of extending a network out to a remote location.

Connect using Direct Connect

AWS Direct Connect is a cloud service solution that makes it easier to establish a dedicated network connection from your premises to AWS. It is a physical line that goes into AWS.

Using Direct Connect, you can establish private connectivity between AWS and your datacenter or office or co-location environment, which (in many cases) can reduce your network costs, increase bandwidth throughput, and provide a more consistent network experience than internet-based connections.

VPN Over Direct Connect

For ultimate security, you can use a VPN over Direct Connect. This means that not only do you have a dedicated line into AWS but also that all your traffic to and from AWS is encrypted over the Direct Connect connection using a VPN.

AWS Lambda

AWS Lambda is a serverless compute service that lets you run code without provisioning or managing servers, creating workload-aware cluster scaling logic, maintaining event integrations, or managing runtimes. With Lambda, you can run code for virtually any type of

application or backend service - all with zero administration.

The Basics of AWS Lambda

The basics of AWS Lambda includes:

- Architecture
- Supported languages
- Pricing
- Version Control
- Shared Responsibility Model

Benefits of AWS Lambda

No servers to manage

AWS Lambda automatically runs your code without requiring you to provision or manage infrastructure.

Continuous scaling

AWS Lambda automatically scales your application by running code in response to each event.

Cost-optimized with millisecond metering

With AWS Lambda, you only pay for the compute time you consume, and you are never paying for over-provisioned infrastructure.

Chapter 04: Billing and Pricing

Introduction

AWS runs with a pay-as-you-go pricing approach for over 70 cloud services. While the number and types of services offered by AWS have increased dramatically, the philosophy of pricing has not changed. At the end of each month, you only pay for what you used in the previous billing period, and you can start or stop using a product at any time. No long-term contracts are required.

AWS is based on the strategy of pricing each service independently to provide customers with remarkable flexibility. This allows them to choose exactly which services they need for their project and to pay only for what they use. AWS pricing is comparable to how you pay for utilities like water or electricity. You only pay for the services consumed with no additional costs or termination fees once you stop using them.

AWS Pricing Policy

Amazon Web Services (AWS) provides a variety of cloud computing services with a utility-style pricing model. For every service, you pay for exactly the amount of resources needed. The following pricing policies apply across AWS for all of the different services it offers:

- Pay as you go
- Pay less when you reserve
- Pay even less per unit by using more
- Pay even less as AWS grows
- Custom pricing

AWS Free Tier

AWS offers a free usage tier to enable new AWS customers to get familiarized with the cloud. A Free Tier account offers the benefit of getting free, hands-on experience with the AWS platform, products and services. Some of the AWS services are free only for the first 12 months while some remain free forever. For example, a new AWS customer can run a free Amazon EC2 Micro Instance for a year while also accessing the free usage tier for Amazon S3, Amazon Elastic Block Store, Amazon Elastic Load Balancing, AWS data transfer and other AWS services.

Free Services

- Amazon VPC
- AWS Elastic Beanstalk
- AWS CloudFormation
- AWS Identity and Access Management (IAM)
- Auto Scaling
- AWS OpsWorks
- Consolidated Billing

Fundamental Pricing Characteristics

Three fundamental characteristics you are charged for:

- Compute
- Storage
- Data Transfer Out

Free Inbound Data Transfer

While Data Transfer Out comes with a price, there is no charge for inbound data transfer across all Amazon Web Services in all regions. In addition, there are no outbound data transfer charges between Amazon Web Services within the same region.

Amazon Elastic Compute Cloud (Amazon EC2)

Amazon EC2 is a web service that enables you to obtain and configure resizable compute capacity in the cloud. Amazon only charges for the computing capacity you actually use. The following factors need to be considered when estimating the cost of using Amazon EC2:

- Clock Hours of Server Time
- Machine Configuration
- Machine Purchase Type
- Number of Instances
- Load Balancing
- Detailed Monitoring
- Auto Scaling
- Elastic IP Addresses
- Operating Systems and Software Packages

Amazon Simple Storage Service (Amazon S3)

Amazon S3 is a web service that provides storage in the cloud. The simple web services interface can be used to store and retrieve any volume of data, at any time, from anywhere on the web. The following factors should be considered when estimating the cost of Amazon S3:

- Storage Class
- Storage
- Requests
- Data Transfer

Amazon Relational Database Service (Amazon RDS)

Amazon RDS is a relational database web service in the cloud that allows you to set up, operate, and scale applications according to your needs. It lets you concentrate on applications and your business by offering cost-efficient and resizable capacity while also handling the database administration tasks. When estimating the cost of Amazon RDS, the following factors need to be considered:

- Clock Hours of Server Time
- Database Characteristics
- Database Purchase Type
- Number of Database Instances
- Provisioned Storage
- Additional Storage
- Requests
- Deployment Type
- Data Transfer

Amazon CloudFront

Amazon CloudFront is a web service for content delivery. It works with other Amazon Web Services to distribute content to end users with low latency and high data transfer speeds, with no minimum commitments. For a cost estimation of Amazon CloudFront, the following factors need to be considered:

- Traffic Distribution
- Requests
- Data Transfer Out

Amazon Elastic Block Store (Amazon EBS)

Amazon EBS offers block level storage volumes to be used with Amazon EC2 instances. These EBS volumes carry on independently, irrespective of the EC2 instance lifespan. They are off-instance storage, similar to virtual disks in the cloud. Amazon EBS offers three types of volume: General Purpose (SSD), Provisioned IOPS (SSD), and Magnetic, all with different costs and performance characteristics.

- Volumes
- Input Output Operations per Second (IOPS)
- Snapshot
- Data Transfer

Saving Further Costs

Different pricing models are available for some of the AWS products, offering you the flexibility to access services according to your requirements:

- **On-Demand Instance** - Pay for compute capacity by the hour, with no minimum commitments required
- **Reserved Instance** - This allows you to reserve compute capacity in advance for long-term savings
- **Spot Instance** - Bid for unused Amazon EC2 capacity. Instances are charged at Spot Price that fluctuates depending on supply and demand

AWS Budgets VS. Cost Explorer

AWS Budgets

AWS Budgets gives you the ability to set custom budgets that alert you when your cost or usage exceeds or is forecasted to exceed your budgeted amount.

It is a way of creating a budget for your AWS account and used to forecast costs before they have been incurred.

AWS Cost Explorer

AWS Cost Explorer is an easy-to-use interface that allows you to visualize, understand, and manage your AWS costs usage over time. It is used to explore costs after they have been incurred.

AWS Support Plans

AWS provides access to tools and expertise under a range of support plans that support the operational health and success of your AWS solutions. You can opt for a support plan according to your organizational requirements; whether you need technical support or additional resources to assist you in planning, deploying and optimizing your AWS environment. AWS offers four

support plans to its customers: Basic, Developer, Business and Enterprise.

- **Basic** – Account you get on Free Tier, offers its customers support for account and billing queries
- **Developer** – offers resources for customers testing or doing early development on AWS
- **Business** – offers resources for customers running production workloads on AWS
- **Enterprise** – offers resources for customers running business & mission-critical workloads on AWS

Comparison of Support Plans

The following tables list the key comparison factors among the four support plans that AWS offers:

Pricing	
Basic	Free
Developer	From $29 per month
Business	From $100 per month
Enterprise	From $15k per month

Technical Support		Technical Account Manager
Basic	-	No
Developer	Business hours access to Cloud Support Associates via email	No
Business	24x7 access to Cloud Support Engineers via email, chat & phone	No
Enterprise	24x7 access to Sr.Cloud Support Engineers via email, chat & phone	Yes

Trusted Advisor	
Basic	Access to 6 core Trusted Advisor checks
Developer	Access to 6 core Trusted Advisor checks
Business	Access to a full set of Trusted Advisor checks
Enterprise	Access to a full set of Trusted Advisor checks

Who can open cases?	
Basic	None
Developer	One prime contact / Unlimited cases
Business	Unlimited contacts / Unlimited cases
Enterprise	Unlimited contacts / Unlimited cases

Case Severity	Response Time	Support Plans
General guidance	< 24 business hours	Developer, Business, and Enterprise
System impaired	< 12 business hours	Developer, Business, and Enterprise
Production system impaired	< 4 hours	Business and Enterprise
Production system down	< 1 hour	Business and Enterprise
Business-critical system down	< 15 minutes	Enterprise Only

Resource Groups and Tagging

Resource Groups

Resource Groups allow you to easily create, maintain, and view a collection of resources that share one or more common tags or portions of tags.

Tags

Tags are words or phrases that act as metadata for identifying and organizing your AWS resources.

AWS Organizations

AWS Organizations is an account management service that allows you to consolidate multiple AWS accounts into an organization, enabling you to create a hierarchical structure that can be managed centrally. Available in two feature sets:

- Only Consolidated billing features – This mode only provides the consolidated billing features

- All features – This mode is the complete feature set that includes all the functionality of consolidated billing in addition to the advanced features that provides more control over the accounts in your organization

Key Features of AWS Organization
- Group-based account management
- Policy framework for multiple AWS accounts
- API level control of AWS services
- Account creation and management APIs
- Consolidated billing
- Enable only consolidated billing features:

Usage of CloudTrial AWS Organizations
CloudTrail is on a per-account basis and is enabled per region. To turn it on for all regions and accounts, you should do the following:

You can consolidate your logs into an S3 bucket by following the given steps:

- Turn Cloud Trial on in your paying account.
- Then, create a bucket policy that allows cross-account access.
- Turn on CloudTrail in all of the other accounts and then use a bucket in the paying account.

Consolidated Billing
Consolidation of the billing of all the AWS accounts in your organization into one bill. Consolidated billing has the following key benefits:

- One Bill – Get one bill for multiple accounts.
- Easy Tracking – Easily track each account's charges.
- Combined Usage – Combine usage from all accounts in the organization results in volume discounts.

AWS QuickStart and Landing Zone
AWS Quick Start
Quick Start is built by AWS solutions architects and AWS Partners to automate reference deployments. There are multiple services available that are designed to provide the environment created by solution architects to help you to get started with a particular technology quickly.

AWS Landing Zone
AWS Landing Zone allows you to set up a multi-account environment with one click. You have your AWS Organizations account, a shared services account, a log Archive account, and a Security account. Therefore, it is going to deploy four different accounts for you. It will go in and set those accounts up. It is a great way of automating multiple accounts. Setting up a multi-account environment can take a vast amount of time due to a large number of design choices. It also requires the configuration of multiple accounts, services and involves a strong understanding of different AWS services.

AWS Partners Program
There are two different types of partners:

- Consulting partners
- Technology partners

Consulting Partners
The consulting partners generally provide a service. This could be designing architecting, building, migrating, and managing customer's workloads and applications on AWS. Therefore, it is sort of service-based and consulting-based.

Technology Partners
Technology partners now provide hardware, connectivity services, or software solutions that are hosted on or integrated with the AWS Cloud.

AWS Cost Calculators
AWS helps you calculate your costs using a couple of calculators:

AWS Simple Monthly Calculator
The AWS Simple Monthly Calculator provides an estimation of your monthly bill depending on your unique configuration of resources. Whether you are running a single instance or dozens of individual services, you can organize your planned resources by service, and the Simple Monthly Calculator will provide you with an estimated cost per month for that configuration.

The calculator provides a per service cost breakdown, as well as an aggregate monthly estimate. You can also use the calculator to see an estimation of and breakdown of costs for common cloud solutions.

AWS TCO (Total Cost of Ownership) Calculator

AWS Total Cost of Ownership (TCO) Calculator provides a comparative analysis of the cost estimation by comparing on-premises and co-location environments to AWS.

It estimates the costs of migrating on-premises infrastructure to AWS and gives you the option to evaluate the savings you would receive if the infrastructure was running on AWS.

Cost Management Using Tags

Tags allow you to add business and organizational statistics to your billing and usage data. You can activate them on the Billing and Cost Management console for cost allocation tracking. AWS provides two types of cost allocation tags

- AWS generated tags
- User-defined tags

Made in United States
North Haven, CT
12 May 2022

19128205R00015